Good Clean Jokes

TO DRIVE YOUR PARENTS CRAZY

Bob Phillips

HARVEST HOUSE PUBLISHERS

EUGENE, OREGON

Cover by Terry Dugan Design, Minneapolis, Minnesota

GOOD CLEAN JOKES TO DRIVE YOUR PARENTS CRAZY

Copyright © 2005 by Bob Phillips
Published by Harvest House Publishers
Eugene, Oregon 97402

ISBN-13: 978-0-7369-1428-4
ISBN-10: 0-7369-1428-5

Printed in the United States of America

07 08 09 10 11 12 13 / BP-MS / 10 9 8 7 6 5 4 3

Crazy Questions

Q: How do you fit six elephants into a car?
A: Put two in the backseat, two in the front seat, one in the glove box, and one in the trunk.

☼ ☼ ☼

Q: How can you double your money quick?
A: Fold it over and put it into your pocket.

☼ ☼ ☼

Q: How does an egg get to work?
A: It drives a yolkswagon.

☼ ☼ ☼

Q: How do you know that dodo birds are smarter than chickens?
A: I'm sure you've never heard of Kentucky Fried Dodo Bird.

※ ※ ※

Q: How many Californians does it take to change a
   lightbulb?
A: None. Californians don't put in lightbulbs; they
   put in hot tubs.

※ ※ ※

Q: How do you turn a beagle into a bird?
A: Remove the *b*.

※ ※ ※

Q: How does an elephant get in a tree?
A: He hides in an acorn and waits for a squirrel to
   carry him up.

※ ※ ※

Q: How do you know that owls are more clever
   than chickens?
A: Have you ever heard of Kentucky Fried Owl?

※ ※ ※

Q: How do you know when perfume is cheap?
A: When you get all you want for a scent.

※ ※ ※

Q: How do you make a pickle laugh?
A: Tell it an elephant joke.

✵ ✵ ✵

Q: How do pigs store their computer files?
A: On sloppy disks.

✵ ✵ ✵

Q: How do you find a missing barber?
A: Comb the city.

✵ ✵ ✵

Q: How do you know when there's an elephant in your chocolate pudding?
A: When it's lumpier than usual.

✵ ✵ ✵

Q: How do you make seven even?
A: Take off the s.

✵ ✵ ✵

Q: How do they put out fires at the post office?
A: They stamp them out.

✵ ✵ ✵

Q: How do you count a herd of cows?
A: With a cowculator.

☀ ☀ ☀

Q: How did they know the invisible man had no children?
A: Because he's not apparent.

☀ ☀ ☀

Q: How do bears walk around?
A: With bear feet.

☀ ☀ ☀

Q: How does the Man in the Moon cut his hair?
A: Eclipse it.

☀ ☀ ☀

Q: How does a mouse feel after it takes a bath?
A: Squeaky-clean.

Wendy & Wesley

Wendy: What's yellow plastic and holds up banks?
Wesley: Search me.
Wendy: A robber duckie.

☼ ☼ ☼

Wendy: What lives at the bottom of the sea, is brightly colored, and is popular around Easter?
Wesley: I'm in the dark.
Wendy: An oyster egg.

☼ ☼ ☼

Wendy: What's big and white and lives in the Sahara Desert?
Wesley: I don't have the foggiest.
Wendy: A lost polar bear.

☼ ☼ ☼

Wendy: What are the last three hairs on a dog's tail called?
Wesley: I'm blank.
Wendy: Dog hairs.

☀ ☀ ☀

Wendy: What is a snake's favorite subject?
Wesley: That's a mystery.
Wendy: SSScience.

☀ ☀ ☀

Wendy: What sits up with a woman when her husband is out late?
Wesley: I have no idea.
Wendy: Her imagination.

☀ ☀ ☀

Wendy: What do you call it when a violin player runs away?
Wesley: I don't know.
Wendy: Fiddler on the hoof.

☀ ☀ ☀

Wendy: What is a liar's favorite month?
Wesley: I pass.
Wendy: Fib-ruary.

☼ ☼ ☼

Wendy: What's the best way to stop a rhinoceros
    from jumping up and down on the bed?
Wesley: Beats me.
Wendy: Put crazy glue on the ceiling.

☼ ☼ ☼

Wendy: What does the government use when it
    takes a census of all the monkeys in the zoo?
Wesley: My mind is a blank.
Wendy: An ape recorder.

☼ ☼ ☼

Wendy: What was Dr. Jekyll's favorite game?
Wesley: Who knows?
Wendy: Hyde-and-Seek.

☼ ☼ ☼

Wendy: What kind of animal always is found at
    baseball games?
Wesley: You tell me.
Wendy: The bat.

☼ ☼ ☼

Wendy: What do you get when you cross a skunk
   with a raccoon?
Wesley: I have no clue.
Wendy: A dirty look from the raccoon.

Wendy: What do you call a bug that arrests other
   bugs?
Wesley: I can't guess.
Wendy: A cop-roach.

Wendy: What happened when the duck was
   arrested?
Wesley: Search me.
Wendy: It quacked under pressure.

Wendy: What do you do if there's a kidnapping in
   Texas?
Wesley: I'm in the dark.
Wendy: Wake him up.

Wendy: What city wanders around aimlessly?
Wesley: I don't have the foggiest.
Wendy: Rome.

✺ ✺ ✺

Wendy: What kind of bird eats the same worm
eight times?
Wesley: I'm blank.
Wendy: A swallow with the hiccups.

✺ ✺ ✺

Wendy: What's the difference between here and
there?
Wesley: That's a mystery.
Wendy: The letter t.

Who's There?

Knock, knock.
Who's there?
Omelette.
Omelette who?
Omelette smarter than I look!

☼ ☼ ☼

Knock, knock.
Who's there?
Divan.
Divan who?
Divan the bathtub and you'll hurt your head.

☼ ☼ ☼

Knock, knock.
Who's there?
Apollo.

Apollo who?
Apologize for not answering sooner!

☀ ☀ ☀

Knock, knock.
Who's there?
Abby.
Abby who?
Abby birthday to you.

☀ ☀ ☀

Knock, knock.
Who's there?
Turnip.
Turnip who?
Turnip the stereo, please.

☀ ☀ ☀

Knock, knock.
Who's there?
Anita.
Anita who?
Anita nother minute to think it over.

☀ ☀ ☀

Knock, knock.
Who's there?
Agatha.
Agatha who?
Agatha headache. Do you have any aspirin?

☀ ☀ ☀

Knock, knock.
Who's there?
Armenia.
Armenia who?
Armenia every word I say.

☀ ☀ ☀

Knock, knock.
Who's there?
Ferdie.
Ferdie who?
Ferdie last time, will you please open the door? My
    foot is still in it.

☀ ☀ ☀

Knock, knock.
Who's there?
Handover.
Handover who?
Hand over your money. This is a stickup.

Knock, knock.
Who's there?
Caesar.
Caesar who?
Caesar jolly good fellow, Caesar jolly good fellow.

Knock, knock.
Who's there?
Hewlett.
Hewlett who?
Hewlett the cat out of the bag?

Knock, knock.
Who's there?
Adele.
Adele who?
Adele is where the farmer's in.

☼ ☼ ☼

Knock, knock.
Who's there?
Thatcher.
Thatcher who?
Thatcher was a funny joke.

Lana &
Lark

Lana: What is the name of the invention that
enables you to see through the thickest walls?
Lark: Search me.
Lana: A window.

※ ※ ※

Lana: What two letters are your teeth afraid of?
Lark: I'm in the dark.
Lana: D-K.

※ ※ ※

Lana: What dreams does a plumber have?
Lark: I'm blank.
Lana: Pipe dreams.

※ ※ ※

Lana: To what kind of party does Frosty the
    Snowman go?
Lark: That's a mystery.
Lana: The snowball.

☀ ☀ ☀

Lana: What do you call three feet of trash?
Lark: I have no idea.
Lana: A junk yard.

☀ ☀ ☀

Lana: What is the best way to take care of a very
    sick pig?
Lark: I don't know.
Lana: Take it to the hospital in a hambulance.

☀ ☀ ☀

Lana: What newspapers do dinosaurs read?
Lark: I pass.
Lana: *The Prehistoric Times.*

☀ ☀ ☀

Lana: What would you get if you crossed a shark
     and a parrot?
Lark: Beats me.
Lana: An animal that talks your ear off.

☀ ☀ ☀

Lana: What is the biggest building in town?
Lark: My mind is a blank.
Lana: The library. It has the most stories.

☀ ☀ ☀

Lana: What did the chickens do in the health club?
Lark: Who knows?
Lana: Eggs-ercise.

☀ ☀ ☀

Lana: What is the quietest sport that is played?
Lark: I give up.
Lana: Bowling, because you can hear a pin drop.

☀ ☀ ☀

Lana: What would you get if you crossed an insect
     and a rabbit?
Lark: You tell me.
Lana: Bugs Bunny.

❀ ❀ ❀

Lana: What goes "peck, peck, peck, bang"?
Lark: I have no clue.
Lana: A chicken in a minefield.

❀ ❀ ❀

Lana: What do you get when you put a jar of honey
    out overnight?
Lark: I can't guess.
Lana: Honeydew.

❀ ❀ ❀

Lana: What is green and always points north?
Lark: Search me.
Lana: A magnetic pickle.

❀ ❀ ❀

Lana: What do frogs wear on their feet in the
    summer?
Lark: I'm in the dark.
Lana: Open-toad shoes.

❀ ❀ ❀

Lana: What wears a mask, smells good, and rides a horse?

Lark: I don't have the foggiest.

Lana: The Cologne Ranger.

☀ ☀ ☀

Lana: What cartoon animal weighs the least?

Lark: I'm blank.

Lana: Skinny the Pooh.

☀ ☀ ☀

Lana: What word if pronounced right is wrong but if pronounced wrong is right?

Lark: That's a mystery.

Lana: *Wrong.*

The
Answer Man

Q: Why was Cinderella such an awful basketball player?

A: She had a pumpkin for a coach.

☀ ☀ ☀

Q: Why is a half-moon heavier than a full moon?

A: A full moon is lighter.

☀ ☀ ☀

Q: Why did the bubble gum cross the road?

A: Because it was stuck to the chicken's foot.

☀ ☀ ☀

Q: Why did the chicken cross the road with an axe?

A: She had an egg there and wanted to hatchet.

※ ※ ※

Q: Why did Colonel Sanders cross the road?
A: He heard there was a chicken on the other side.

※ ※ ※

Q: Why did the cow enroll in drama class?
A: To become a moo-vie star.

※ ※ ※

Q: Why didn't the skeleton go to the dance?
A: Because he had no body to go with.

※ ※ ※

Q: Why did the worm cross the road?
A: The chicken was chasing it.

※ ※ ※

Q: Why was the chiropractor upset?
A: All he got from his patients was back talk.

※ ※ ※

Q: Why was the fox upset?
A: Everyone kept hounding him.

※ ※ ※

Q: Why did the dinosaur cross the road?
A: Because in those days they didn't have chickens.

☼ ☼ ☼

Q: Why did the elephant lie in the middle of the road?
A: To trip the ants.

☼ ☼ ☼

Q: Why don't fish go on-line?
A: Because they're afraid of being caught in the Net.

☼ ☼ ☼

Q: Why did the giant squids get such low grades?
A: They couldn't ink straight.

☼ ☼ ☼

Q: Why wouldn't the lemon help the orange?
A: It could sour their friendship.

☼ ☼ ☼

Q: Why didn't the burrito cross the road?
A: It was too chicken.

☼ ☼ ☼

Q: Why did the police question the burrito?
A: So he would spill the beans.

☼ ☼ ☼

Q: Why did the clown go to the doctor?
A: He was feeling a little funny.

When, When, When

Garrett: When you fill me up, I still look empty.
    What am I?
Gary: Search me.
Garrett: A balloon.

☼ ☼ ☼

Sandy: When my little girl got married, I didn't lose
    a daughter; I gained a goofy son.
Sally: What do you mean?
Sandy: He moved in with us.

☼ ☼ ☼

Monica: When is it right for you to lie?
Melanie: I'm in the dark.
Monica: When you are in bed.

☼ ☼ ☼

Cole: When are people very glad to be down-and-out?

Joel: I don't have the foggiest.

Cole: After a bumpy plane trip.

☼ ☼ ☼

Mandie: When a pig writes a letter, what does it use?

Meagan: I'm blank.

Mandie: Pen and oink.

☼ ☼ ☼

Anna: When farmers want to start a race, what do they say?

Amy: It's a mystery to me.

Anna: Ready, set . . . hoe!

☼ ☼ ☼

James: When chickens become ghosts, what sound do they make?

Jim: I have no idea.

James: Peck-a-boo.

☼ ☼ ☼

Hannah: When is an elevator not an elevator?
Seth: I don't know.
Hannah: When it is going down.

☼ ☼ ☼

Jack: When can you see yourself in a place you've
never been?
Katie: I pass.
Jack: When you look into a mirror.

☼ ☼ ☼

Ben: When you order bison steaks at a restaurant,
what does the waiter bring you after the meal?
Echo: Beats me.
Ben: A Buffalo Bill.

☼ ☼ ☼

Carrie: When a girl slips and falls while roller-
skating, why can't her brother help her up?
Jamie: My mind is a blank.
Carrie: He can't be a brother and assist her, too.

☼ ☼ ☼

Sidney: When a dog graduates from obedience
    school, what does he get?
Leroy: Who knows?
Sidney: A pet-degree.

☼ ☼ ☼

Lisa: When the chicken forgot its lines in the
    school play, what did Barbie, the dramatics
    teacher, do to help?
Christy: I give up.
Lisa: Barbie cued the chicken.

☼ ☼ ☼

Richard: When a lemon calls for help, what does it
    want?
Kimberly: You tell me.
Richard: Lemonade.

Chip & Chuck

Chip: What do you call a nut that never remembers?

Chuck: Search me.

Chip: A forget-me-nut.

☼ ☼ ☼

Chip: What part of London is in France?

Chuck: I'm in the dark.

Chip: The letter *n*.

☼ ☼ ☼

Chip: What did the dirt say when it rained?

Chuck: I don't have the foggiest.

Chip: "If this keeps up, my name is mud."

☼ ☼ ☼

Chip: What is the strangest kind of commercial?
Chuck: I'm blank.
Chip: An odd-vertisement.

☀ ☀ ☀

Chip: What did the bald man say when he got a
comb for a gift?
Chuck: That's a mystery.
Chip: I'll never part with it.

☀ ☀ ☀

Chip: What do you get when you cross a stream
and a brook?
Chuck: I have no idea.
Chip: Wet feet.

☀ ☀ ☀

Chip: What trees are left behind after a fire?
Chuck: I don't know.
Chip: Ashes.

☀ ☀ ☀

Chip: What do cows wear when they're vacationing
in Hawaii?
Chuck: I pass.
Chip: Moo-moos.

☼ ☼ ☼

Chip: What kind of lizard loves riddles?
Chuck: Beats me.
Chip: A sillymander.

☼ ☼ ☼

Chip: What kind of cow goes "beeeeep, beeeeep"?
Chuck: My mind is a blank.
Chip: A longhorn.

☼ ☼ ☼

Chip: What do magicians say on Halloween?
Chuck: Who knows?
Chip: "Trick or trick!"

☼ ☼ ☼

Chip: What would you hear at a cow concert?
Chuck: I give up.
Chip: Moo-sic.

☼ ☼ ☼

Chip: What did the silly comedian bake on his day
   off?
Chuck: You tell me.
Chip: Corn bread.

Chip: What two members of the cow family go
   everywhere with you?
Chuck: I have no clue.
Chip: Your calves.

Chip: What amusement-park ride is only 12 inches
   long?
Chuck: I can't guess.
Chip: A ruler coaster.

Chip: What animal eats with its tail?
Chuck: Search me.
Chip: They all do. They can't take them off.

Chip: What do you need to know to teach tricks to
    a grasshopper?
Chuck: I'm in the dark.
Chip: More than the grasshopper.

☼ ☼ ☼

Chip: What did the chewing gum say to the shoe?
Chuck: I don't have the foggiest.
Chip: "I'm stuck on you."

☼ ☼ ☼

Chip: What happens when you irritate a clock?
Chuck: I'm blank.
Chip: It gets ticked off.

☼ ☼ ☼

Chip: What animal drops from the clouds?
Chuck: That's a mystery.
Chip: The rain, dear.

Teachers

Teacher: Who is Isaac Newton?
Student: I have no idea, but I've heard of his
　　brother, Fig.

※ ※ ※

Teacher: I hope I didn't see you copying the test
　　from your friend.
Student: I hope you didn't, too.

※ ※ ※

Teacher: How do you make Mexican chili?
Student: Take him to the North Pole.

※ ※ ※

Teacher: Name the four seasons.
Student: Track, football, basketball, baseball.

※ ※ ※

Teacher: Are you good at English?
Student: Yes and no.
Teacher: What do you mean by that?
Student: Yes, I'm no good at English.

☼ ☼ ☼

Teacher: A fool can ask more questions than a wise man can answer.
Student: No wonder so many of us flunk our exams.

☼ ☼ ☼

Teacher: Why didn't you turn in your homework?
Student: I was going to, but on the way to school I saw a boy in a lake and I jumped in to rescue him and my homework drowned.

☼ ☼ ☼

Teacher: Where does satisfaction come from?
Student: A satisfactory.

☼ ☼ ☼

Teacher: Why is the school basketball court always so soggy?
Student: Because the players are always dribbling.

☀ ☀ ☀

Teacher: Now, before we go out for recess, I want
    you to answer some questions. Remember, all of
    your responses must be oral. Do you under-
    stand?
Student: Oral.
Teacher: How many letters are there in the
    alphabet?
Student: Oral.

☀ ☀ ☀

Teacher: Please give me an example of a double
    negative.
Student: I don't know none.
Teacher: Correct, thank you!

Gaylord & Gladys

Gaylord: What is a mouse's favorite game?
Gladys: Search me.
Gaylord: Hide-and-squeak.

☼ ☼ ☼

Gaylord: What do you call two hornets, a wasp, and
    a bee that play musical instruments?
Gladys: I'm in the dark.
Gaylord: A sting quartet.

☼ ☼ ☼

Gaylord: What happened when the doctor told a
    joke during surgery?
Gladys: I don't have the foggiest.
Gaylord: The patient was left in stitches.

☼ ☼ ☼

Gaylord: What happens when you ask an oyster a
    personal question?
Gladys: I'm blank.
Gaylord: It clams up.

☀ ☀ ☀

Gaylord: What do you get from pampered cows?
Gladys: That's a mystery.
Gaylord: Spoiled milk.

☀ ☀ ☀

Gaylord: What does Mickey Mouse's girlfriend
    wear?
Gladys: I have no idea.
Gaylord: Minnie skirts.

☀ ☀ ☀

Gaylord: What do cows do when they're introduced?
Gladys: I don't know.
Gaylord: They give each other a milk shake.

☀ ☀ ☀

Gaylord: What is the name of the saddest bird
    alive?
Gladys: I pass.
Gaylord: The bluebird.

☼ ☼ ☼

Gaylord: What kind of bulls giggle?
Gladys: Beats me.
Gaylord: Laughingstock.

☼ ☼ ☼

Gaylord: What a cute little boy! What is your
    name, sweetheart?
Gladys: Connor.
Gaylord: Can you tell me your full name?
Gladys: Connor Stop That!

☼ ☼ ☼

Gaylord: What do you get when you cross a black
    cat with a yo-yo?
Gladys: My mind is a blank.
Gaylord: A string of bad luck.

☼ ☼ ☼

Gaylord: What do they call a monkey that sells
    potato chips?
Gladys: I give up.
Gaylord: A chip monk.

☼ ☼ ☼

Gaylord: What pen is never used for writing?
Gladys: I have no clue.
Gaylord: A pigpen.

☼ ☼ ☼

Gaylord: What happens to a deer when an archer
   shoots at it and misses?
Gladys: I can't guess.
Gaylord: It has an arrow escape.

☼ ☼ ☼

Gaylord: What happens when a chimpanzee twists
   his ankle?
Gladys: Search me.
Gaylord: He gets a monkey wrench.

☼ ☼ ☼

Gaylord: What are people who ride on Greyhound
   buses called?
Gladys: I'm in the dark.
Gaylord: Passengers.

☼ ☼ ☼

Gaylord: What time is it when an elephant sits on
   your fence?
Gladys: I don't have the foggiest.
Gaylord: Time to buy a new fence.

☼ ☼ ☼

Gaylord: What puts the white lines on the ocean?
Gladys: I'm blank.
Gaylord: An ocean liner.

Friends

Debs: When is a pink elephant most likely to enter a classroom?
Jerry: Search me.
Debs: When the door's open.

☼ ☼ ☼

Jan: Who is radioactive and wears a mask?
Bud: I'm in the dark.
Jan: The Glowin' Ranger.

☼ ☼ ☼

Eve: Is that a pleasant highway to drive on?
Steve: No, it's a crossroad.

☼ ☼ ☼

Josh: Do you know why the Statue of Liberty
    stands in New York harbor?
Jim: I'm blank.
Josh: Because it can't sit down.

☼ ☼ ☼

Pilgrim William: Why did Pilgrim James eat a
    candle, pray tell?
Pilgrim Daniel: That's a mystery.
Pilgrim William: I understand he was not very
    hungry and only wanted a light snack.

☼ ☼ ☼

Ian: Who cut your hair that way?
P.K.: My barber.
Ian: What did he use?
P.K.: He used a sword.
Ian: What is his name?
P.K.: Conan the barberian.

☼ ☼ ☼

Nit: I've forgotten everything I ever learned.
Wit: Well, what do you know?

☼ ☼ ☼

Jonnie: Why did the banana go out with the prune?
Becky: I have no idea.
Jonnie: It couldn't get a date.

☼ ☼ ☼

Sheila: Who was the girl in the story that put her
    foot into a glass slipper and, in the process,
    smashed it to pieces?
Ray: I don't know.
Sheila: Cinder-elephant.

☼ ☼ ☼

Burt: Why does my pet spider like to use my com-
    puter so much?
Kurt: I pass.
Burt: It likes to check out web sites.

☼ ☼ ☼

Pam: You should hear my new portable radio. Last
    night I got Mexico.
Sam: That's nothing. I just opened the window and
    got Chile.

☼ ☼ ☼

Junior: Dad, I can't find my baseball mitt.
Dad: Look in the car.
Junior: I did, but I couldn't find it.
Dad: Did you try the glove compartment?

☼ ☼ ☼

Igor: I trace my ancestors all the way back to royalty.
Boris: King Kong?

☼ ☼ ☼

Gertrude: Who has six legs, wears a coonskin cap,
     and chirps?
Gerard: Beats me.
Gertrude: Davy Cricket.

☼ ☼ ☼

Mike: I went to Switzerland on my vacation.
Mick: Really? What did you think of the scenery?
Mike: Oh, I couldn't see much. There were all
     those mountains in the way.

☼ ☼ ☼

Tim: You slept under the car during your vacation?
     Why?
Jim: I wanted to get up oily in the morning!

☀ ☀ ☀

Son: Pop, I can tell you how to save money.
Father: That's fine. How?
Son: Remember you promised me five dollars if I
    got passing grades?
Father: Yes.
Son: Well, you don't have to pay me.

☀ ☀ ☀

Tina: What's your job at the weight reduction
    clinic?
Gina: I work in middle management.

☀ ☀ ☀

Jen: How is the Internet like an overgrown yard?
Len: You have to modem both.

☀ ☀ ☀

Patsy: Who was the first man to make a monkey of
    himself?
Norm: My mind is a blank.
Patsy: Darwin.

Bertram &
Blossom

Bertram: What do you call a dog who sleeps on top of your computer?
Blossom: Search me.
Bertram: Browser.

☼ ☼ ☼

Bertram: What do you get if you cross an old clock with a chicken?
Blossom: I'm in the dark.
Bertram: A grandfather cluck.

☼ ☼ ☼

Bertram: What boy likes to lay in front of the door?
Blossom: I don't have the foggiest.
Bertram: Matt.

☀ ☀ ☀

Bertram: What bone can't a dog eat?
Blossom: I'm blank.
Bertram: A trombone.

☀ ☀ ☀

Bertram: What would you get if you put a lightbulb
  in a suit of armor?
Blossom: That's a mystery.
Bertram: A knight-light.

☀ ☀ ☀

Bertram: What do people in Tibet do when it rains?
Blossom: I have no idea.
Bertram: They let it rain.

☀ ☀ ☀

Bertram: What did one elevator say to the other
  elevator?
Blossom: I don't know.
Bertram: I think I'm coming down with something.

☀ ☀ ☀

Bertram: What is the distance between the ears of a very, very stupid person?
Blossom: I pass.
Bertram: Next to nothing.

☼ ☼ ☼

Bertram: What do you call a dog with no legs?
Blossom: Beats me.
Bertram: It doesn't really matter. It won't come anyway.

☼ ☼ ☼

Bertram: What kind of umbrella does the president of Canada carry on a rainy day?
Blossom: My mind is a blank.
Bertram: A wet one.

☼ ☼ ☼

Bertram: What is the best way to see flying saucers?
Blossom: Who knows?
Bertram: Scare the waitress.

Bertram: What is the name of the laziest mountain in all the world?

Blossom: I give up.

Bertram: Mount Everest.

※ ※ ※

Bertram: What is the difference between a doormat and a medicine bottle?

Blossom: You tell me.

Bertram: One is taken up and shaken, the other is shaken up and taken.

※ ※ ※

Bertram: What do they call someone who can stick to a reducing diet?

Blossom: I have no clue.

Bertram: A good loser.

※ ※ ※

Bertram: What is a comedian's favorite breakfast cereal?

Blossom: I can't guess.

Bertram: Cream of wit.

※ ※ ※

Bertram: What did Mr. Bird call his son?
Blossom: Search me.
Bertram: A chirp off the old block.

☀ ☀ ☀

Bertram: What do rabbits sing to each other once a
year?
Blossom: I'm in the dark.
Bertram: "Hoppy Birthday."

☀ ☀ ☀

Bertram: What university do dogs go to?
Blossom: I don't have the foggiest.
Bertram: Bark-ley.

☀ ☀ ☀

Bertram: What do you get when you put too much
mousse on your head?
Blossom: I'm blank.
Bertram: Antlers.

Open the Door!

Knock, knock.
Who's there?
Judy.
Judy who?
Judyliver newspapers still?

☼ ☼ ☼

Knock, knock.
Who's there?
Luke.
Luke who?
Luke both ways before crossing.

☼ ☼ ☼

Knock, knock.
Who's there?
Police.

Police who?
Police open the door.

❀ ❀ ❀

Knock, knock.
Who's there?
Radio.
Radio who?
Radio not, here I come.

❀ ❀ ❀

Knock, knock.
Who's there?
Enoch.
Enoch who?
Enoch and Enoch but nobody opens the door.

❀ ❀ ❀

Knock, knock.
Who's there?
Wednesday.
Wednesday who?
Wednesday saints go marching in . . .

✿ ✿ ✿

Knock, knock.
Who's there?
Who Who.
Who Who who?
You sound like an owl.

✿ ✿ ✿

Knock, knock.
Who's there?
Turnip.
Turnip who?
Turnip the heat. It's cold in the house.

✿ ✿ ✿

Knock, knock.
Who's there?
Zippy.
Zippy who?
Zippy de do da . . . zippy de day . . . my, oh my, what
    a wonderful day.

✿ ✿ ✿

Knock, knock.
Who's there?
Walter.
Walter who?
Walter-wall carpeting for sale. Would you like some?

☀ ☀ ☀

Knock, knock.
Who's there?
Ella.
Ella who?
Ella-vator. Doesn't that give you a lift?

☀ ☀ ☀

Knock, knock.
Who's there?
Avenue.
Avenue who?
Avenue been missing me?

☀ ☀ ☀

Knock, knock.
Who's there?
Oscar and Greta.
Oscar and Greta who?
Oscar foolish question, Greta foolish answer.

Winthrop & Whitney

Winthrop: What does the Lone Ranger say when he drops off his garbage?
Whitney: Search me.
Winthrop: To-de-dump, to-de-dump, to-de-dump-dump-dump.

※ ※ ※

Winthrop: What's the name of the bestselling biography of 400 famous owls?
Whitney: I'm in the dark.
Winthrop: *Who's Who.*

※ ※ ※

Winthrop: What is the most popular game show for fish?
Whitney: I don't have the foggiest.
Winthrop: "Name That Tuna."

☀ ☀ ☀

Winthrop: What kind of berry always seems sad?
Whitney: I'm blank.
Winthrop: A blue-berry.

☀ ☀ ☀

Winthrop: What do they call a Santa Claus who
    drops the presents all the time?
Whitney: That's a mystery.
Winthrop: Santa Klutz.

☀ ☀ ☀

Winthrop: What do you get if you cross a pig and a
    red light?
Whitney: I have no idea.
Winthrop: A stop swine.

☀ ☀ ☀

Winthrop: What do they call a prehistoric skunk?
Whitney: I don't know.
Winthrop: Ex-stinct.

☀ ☀ ☀

Winthrop: What do they call an eye that goes to
   school?
Whitney: I pass.
Winthrop: The pupil.

Winthrop: What is as big as an elephant but
   doesn't weigh anything?
Whitney: Beats me.
Winthrop: The shadow of an elephant.

Winthrop: What does a kangaroo eat at the
   movies?
Whitney: My mind is a blank.
Winthrop: Hop-corn.

Winthrop: What is the first word a baby computer
   says?
Whitney: Who knows?
Winthrop: *Da-ta.*

Winthrop: What do you get if you cross a worm
    with an elephant?
Whitney: I give up.
Winthrop: Big holes in your garden.

☀ ☀ ☀

Winthrop: What do they call a lumberjack who fells
    trees and shouts too late?
Whitney: You tell me.
Winthrop: Tim.

☀ ☀ ☀

Winthrop: What's a cow's favorite love song?
Whitney: I have no clue.
Winthrop: "When I Fall in Love, It Will Be for
    Heifer."

☀ ☀ ☀

Winthrop: What is one and one?
Whitney: Two.
Winthrop: What is four minus two?
Whitney: Two.
Winthrop: Who wrote Tom Sawyer?
Whitney: Twain.
Winthrop: Now say all the answers together.

Whitney: Two, two, Twain.
Winthrop: Have a nice trip.

☀ ☀ ☀

Winthrop: What is the laziest shoe?
Whitney: I can't guess.
Winthrop: A loafer.

☀ ☀ ☀

Winthrop: What song do you usually hear bees
    singing?
Whitney: Search me.
Winthrop: "Stinging in the Rain."

☀ ☀ ☀

Winthrop: What should you do if you find a 500-
    pound shaggy dog wearing your favorite tie?
Whitney: I'm in the dark.
Winthrop: Go see a doctor. You have been seeing
    entirely too many 500-pound shaggy dogs
    lately.

☀ ☀ ☀

Winthrop: What belongs to you, but other people use it more than you do?
Whitney: I don't have the foggiest.
Winthrop: Your name.

☀ ☀ ☀

Winthrop: What cowboy wears a black mask just like the Lone Ranger's, rides a horse just like Silver, and has a sidekick who could be Tonto's twin brother?
Whitney: I'm blank.
Winthrop: The Clone Ranger.

Questions & Answers

Q: Why did the frog cross the road?
A: She was stapled to the chicken.

☀ ☀ ☀

Q: Why do they call him Mumps?
A: Because he's a swell guy.

☀ ☀ ☀

Q: Why did the children play Kick the Pebble?
A: Because it was too hard to play Kick the Boulder.

☀ ☀ ☀

Q: Why do firemen slide down a pole in the fire-
   house?
A: Because it's too hard to slide up.

☀ ☀ ☀

Q: Why did the composer spend all his time in bed?

A: He wrote sheet music.

※ ※ ※

Q: Why are skunks good decision-makers?

A: Because they have a lot of common scents.

※ ※ ※

Q: Why do traffic lights make people angry?

A: Every time the lights turn green, they make you cross.

※ ※ ※

Q: Why did the man put a television set in his laundry room?

A: He needed a new watching machine.

※ ※ ※

Q: Why was the farmer cross?

A: Because someone stepped on his corn.

※ ※ ※

Q: Why does that weird man take a bale of hay to bed with him?

A: To feed his nightmares.

☼ ☼ ☼

Q: Why do teachers think they are so special?

A: Because they think they are in a class of their own.

☼ ☼ ☼

Q: Why did the germ cross the microscope?

A: To get to the other slide.

☼ ☼ ☼

Q: Why do plumbers wear yellow suspenders?

A: To keep their pants up.

Tongue Twisters

Charlie Chisim chomps cheap charcoal cherries.

☀ ☀ ☀

Mixed biscuits boxed badly are mixed by the biscuit mixer.

☀ ☀ ☀

Sally sells sick snails smelling salts.

☀ ☀ ☀

Seven shameful sharks slashed satin sheets.

☀ ☀ ☀

Silly shapeless sashes sag sadly.

☀ ☀ ☀

Simeon's slippery ship is shipshape, sir.

☼ ☼ ☼

Sixty-six shy sick sticky snakes slithered silently.

☼ ☼ ☼

She said Suzie sheared six shabby sheep slowly.

☼ ☼ ☼

Should selfish Sheriff Sam Short sup soup at cheap
chop suey shops?

☼ ☼ ☼

Shy sly slim Sheriff Shultz slays seven sly shy slith-
ering snakes. .

☼ ☼ ☼

Take the cheap silly ship trip.

☼ ☼ ☼

Zelda sews zither covers.

Leonard &
Leona

Leonard: What kind of player gives refunds?
Leona: I'm in the dark.
Leonard: A quarterback.

☀ ☀ ☀

Leonard: What do you call a tomato that insults a
farmer?
Leona: I don't have the foggiest.
Leonard: A very fresh vegetable.

☀ ☀ ☀

Leonard: What is a shaggy dog who crosses the
street twice in an hour?
Leona: I'm blank.
Leonard: A double-crosser.

☀ ☀ ☀

Leonard: What is the favorite breakfast food of
cats?
Leona: That's a mystery.
Leonard: Mice Crispies.

Leonard: What do you get if you cross a karate
expert with a tree?
Leona: I have no idea.
Leonard: Spruce Lee.

Leonard: What is the difference between a
postage stamp and a girl?
Leona: I don't know.
Leonard: One is a mail fee and the other is a
female.

Leonard: What was Noah's profession?
Leona: I pass.
Leonard: He was an ark-itect.

Leonard: What is sweet, comes in different flavors
    and colors, and makes music?
Leona: Beats me.
Leonard: Cello pudding.

☼ ☼ ☼

Leonard: What kind of letters did the snake get
    from his admirers?
Leona: My mind is a blank.
Leonard: Fang mail.

☼ ☼ ☼

Leonard: What goes in one ear and out the other?
Leona: Who knows?
Leonard: A worm in a cornfield.

☼ ☼ ☼

Leonard: What do you get when you cross a hen
    with a banjo?
Leona: I give up.
Leonard: A chicken that plays a tune when you
    pluck it.

Leonard: What kind of trains do ballerinas take?
Leona: You tell me.
Leonard: Tutu trains.

☼ ☼ ☼

Leonard: What is the best thing to do when you
don't feel well?
Leona: I have no clue.
Leonard: Take off your gloves.

☼ ☼ ☼

Leonard: What do angels say when they answer
the telephone?
Leona: I can't guess.
Leonard: "Halo!"

☼ ☼ ☼

Leonard: What would happen if you cut your left
side off?
Leona: Search me.
Leonard: You'd be all right.

☼ ☼ ☼

Leonard: What did one tree say to the other tree at
the end of the day?
Leona: I'm in the dark.
Leonard: "I've gotta leave!"

☼ ☼ ☼

Leonard: What did the painter say to the wall?
Leona: I don't have the foggiest.
Leonard: "One more crack like that and I'll plaster
you."

☼ ☼ ☼

Leonard: What do you get when you put a bird in
the freezer?
Leona: I'm blank.
Leonard: A brrrd.

What If?

Q: If you had a splitting headache, what would be the best thing to take?

A: Glue-covered aspirin.

☀ ☀ ☀

Q: If a lawyer was hurt in a swimming pool, what kind of court case would he bring?

A: A bathing suit.

☀ ☀ ☀

Q: If you try to cross a lake in a leaky boat, what do you get?

A: About halfway.

☀ ☀ ☀

Q: If you cross a Boy Scout with a kangaroo, what do you get?

A: A kangaroo that helps old ladies hop across the street.

☀ ☀ ☀

Q: If you see the handwriting on the wall, what
    does that mean?
A: That there's a child in the family.

☀ ☀ ☀

Q: If you cross a germ with a comedian, what do
    you get?
A: A lot of sick jokes.

☀ ☀ ☀

Q: If 16 girls share a chocolate cake, what time is
    it?
A: A quarter to four.

☀ ☀ ☀

Q: If it takes 13 men 11 days to dig a hole, how long
    will it take 7 men to dig half a hole?
A: There is no such thing as half a hole.

☀ ☀ ☀

Q: If a man rides to a farm on Friday and stays four
    days, how can he ride out on Friday?
A: Friday is the name of his horse.

☀ ☀ ☀

Q: If a papa bull eats five bales of hay, and a baby bull eats one bale of hay, how many bales of hay will a mama bull eat?

A: There is no such thing as a mama bull.

☀ ☀ ☀

Q: If someone hits you in the head with an ax, what do you get?

A: A splitting headache.

Gertrude &
Gerhard

Gertrude: What do you call a cat who eats a pickle?
Gerhard: Search me.
Gertrude: A pickle puss!

☼ ☼ ☼

Gertrude: What song did they play when the
cookie got married?
Gerhard: I don't have the foggiest.
Gertrude: "Here Crumbs the Bride."

☼ ☼ ☼

Gertrude: What do you call a formal dance for
butchers?
Gerhard: I'm blank.
Gertrude: A meatball.

☼ ☼ ☼

Gertrude: What kind of bath can you take without water?

Gerhard: That's a mystery.

Gertrude: A sunbath.

☼ ☼ ☼

Gertrude: What kinds of animals can jump higher than the Statue of Liberty?

Gerhard: I have no idea.

Gertrude: Any kind. The Statue of Liberty can't jump.

☼ ☼ ☼

Gertrude: What do you get if you tie two bicycles together?

Gerhard: I pass.

Gertrude: Siamese Schwinns.

☼ ☼ ☼

Gertrude: What did the hog say when he heard a pig joke?

Gerhard: Beats me.

Gertrude: "Now that's squeally funny."

Gertrude: What do you call it when five toads sit
   on top of each other?
Gerhard: My mind is a blank.
Gertrude: A toad-em pole.

☀ ☀ ☀

Gertrude: What do computers get paid to do?
Gerhard: Who knows?
Gertrude: Network.

☀ ☀ ☀

Gertrude: What do you call the boss at a dairy?
Gerhard: I give up.
Gertrude: The big cheese.

☀ ☀ ☀

Gertrude: What hops up in the morning and
   crows?
Gerhard: You tell me.
Gertrude: A kanga-rooster.

☀ ☀ ☀

Gertrude: What do you call a piece of popcorn that joins the Army?
Gerhard: I have no clue.
Gertrude: Kernel.

☀ ☀ ☀

Gertrude: What big cat lives in people's backyards?
Gerhard: I can't guess.
Gertrude: A clothes lion.

☀ ☀ ☀

Gertrude: What is a rowboat's favorite state?
Gerhard: Search me.
Gertrude: Oar-egon.

☀ ☀ ☀

Gertrude: What do you call a formal dance for turkeys?
Gerhard: I'm in the dark.
Gertrude: A turkey trot.

☀ ☀ ☀

Gertrude: What do you call a flying ape?
Gerhard: I don't have the foggiest.
Gertrude: A hot-air baboon.

※ ※ ※

Gertrude: What cereal goes "snap, crackle,
    squeak"?
Gerhard: I'm blank.
Gertrude: Mice Krispies.

School

Teacher: What kind of leather makes the best shoes?

Student: I don't know, but banana peels make the best slippers.

Teacher: Why were you late in getting to school?

Student: I overslept.

Teacher: You mean that you sleep at home, too?

☼ ☼ ☼

Teacher: Please tell me where your right foot was located when you fell down and got hurt.

Student: My right foot was located at the end of my right leg.

☼ ☼ ☼

Teacher: What can you tell me about the Dead Sea?

Student: Gee whiz, I didn't even know it was sick!

❀ ❀ ❀

Teacher: What did you learn in school today?

Student: How to whisper without moving my lips.

❀ ❀ ❀

Teacher: What is the highest form of animal life?

Student: The giraffe.

❀ ❀ ❀

Teacher: What do you call the last teeth we get?

Student: False teeth.

❀ ❀ ❀

Teacher: Why are you late for school this time?

Student: I sprained my ankle running to the bus.

Teacher: That's a lame excuse.

❀ ❀ ❀

Teacher: My education was dismal.
Student: Why do you say that?
Teacher: I went to a series of schools for mentally
  disturbed teachers.

☀ ☀ ☀

One day in school the teacher wrote on the black-
  board, "I ain't had no fun at all last week." She
  turned to her class and said, "Now what should I
  do to correct that?"
A shy student stood up and replied meekly, "Maybe
  you should get a boyfriend."

☀ ☀ ☀

When a teacher calls a boy by his entire name it
  means trouble.
                          —Mark Twain

☀ ☀ ☀

A professor is one who talks in someone else's
  sleep.

☀ ☀ ☀

My teacher has a reading problem. He can't read
my writing.

—Leopold Fechtner

Coco & Connor

Coco: What besides a supersonic jet goes faster than the speed of sound?
Connor: Search me.
Coco: My Aunt Gladys when she talks.

☀ ☀ ☀

Coco: What happened to the computer when it crashed?
Connor: I'm in the dark.
Coco: It got a slipped disk.

☀ ☀ ☀

Coco: What is easier to give than to receive?
Connor: I don't have the foggiest.
Coco: Criticism.

☀ ☀ ☀

Coco: What's a pig's favorite music?
Connor: I'm blank.
Coco: Hip-slop.

☀ ☀ ☀

Coco: What do you call a cat with a pager?
Connor: That's a mystery.
Coco: A beeping tom.

☀ ☀ ☀

Coco: What do you say to an electrician?
Connor: I have no idea.
Coco: "Thanks a watt!"

☀ ☀ ☀

Coco: What causes the most noise in space?
Connor: I don't know.
Coco: Shooting stars.

☀ ☀ ☀

Coco: What is a gorilla's favorite drink?
Connor: I pass.
Coco: Lemon-ape.

☀ ☀ ☀

Coco: What is the politest thing to say when you are introduced to a road?

Connor: Beats me.

Coco: "Hi, way!"

Coco: What do you call popcorn kernels that don't pop?

Connor: My mind is a blank.

Coco: Flop-corn.

Coco: What did one car muffler say to the other car muffler?

Connor: Who knows?

Coco: "Boy, am I exhausted!"

Coco: What would you get if you crossed a bronco with a dog?

Connor: I give up.

Coco: An animal whose buck is worse than his bite.

Coco: What did the tire jack say to the car?
Connor: You tell me.
Coco: "Can I give you a lift?"

☼ ☼ ☼

Coco: What's a computer's favorite snack?
Connor: I have no clue.
Coco: Chips.

☼ ☼ ☼

Coco: What is the name for a knight who is caught in a very bad windstorm?
Connor: I can't guess.
Coco: Nightingale.

☼ ☼ ☼

Coco: What insect keeps good time?
Connor: Search me.
Coco: A clock-roach.

☼ ☼ ☼

Coco: What did the beaver say to the aspen tree?
Connor: I'm in the dark.
Coco: "It's been nice gnawing you."

☀ ☀ ☀

Coco: What is the best kind of letter to read on a
    hot day?
Connor: I don't have the foggiest.
Coco: Fan mail.

☀ ☀ ☀

Coco: What kind of apple isn't an apple?
Connor: I'm blank.
Coco: A pineapple.

Where, Oh Where?

Q: Where do you take a sick ocean liner?
A: To the dock.

☼ ☼ ☼

Q: Where does the sandman like to keep his sleeping sand?
A: In his knapsack.

☼ ☼ ☼

Q: Where do fish like to go for vacation?
A: Finland.

☼ ☼ ☼

Q: Where do old Volkswagen cars end up?
A: In the old Volks home.

☼ ☼ ☼

Q: Where is the capital of the United States?
A: All over the world.

✺ ✺ ✺

Q: Where does a dog sleep when it's camping?
A: In a pup tent!

✺ ✺ ✺

Q: Where should you put your TV?
A: In a remote area.

✺ ✺ ✺

Q: Where do penguins keep their money?
A: In a snowbank.

✺ ✺ ✺

Q: Where do they serve snacks to football players?
A: In the Soup-er Bowl.

✺ ✺ ✺

Q: Where is the largest diamond in the world found?
A: On a baseball field.

☼ ☼ ☼

Q: Where do otters come from?
A: Otter space.

☼ ☼ ☼

Q: Where do fish wash themselves?
A: In bass-tubs.

☼ ☼ ☼

Q: Where do bow ties go on vacation?
A: To Thailand.

☼ ☼ ☼

Q: Where did the chicken go on her vacation?
A: To Sandy Eggo.

☼ ☼ ☼

Q: Where is the best place to see a man-eating fish?
A: At a seafood restaurant.

☼ ☼ ☼

Q: Where do jellyfish sleep?
A: In tent-acles.

☼ ☼ ☼

Q: Where do sea horses sleep?
A: Near barn-acles.

☼ ☼ ☼

Q: Where did King Arthur study for his math test?
A: In Cram-a-lot.

☼ ☼ ☼

Q: Where did Tarzan go on his vacation?
A: To Hollywood & Vine.

☼ ☼ ☼

Q: Where are most turkeys found?
A: Between the head and the tail.

☼ ☼ ☼

Q: Where do all the jungle animals like to eat lunch?
A: At the beastro.

☀ ☀ ☀

Q: Where do pizzas like to vacation?
A: In Florida, so they can bake.

More Friends

Milo: My uncle's wife is an astronaut.
Philo: Wow, talk about Auntie Gravity.

☼ ☼ ☼

Wes: How do you make a crème puff?
Les: Chase it around the block a few times.

☼ ☼ ☼

Joe: What do you get when you cross a turkey with a banjo?
Moe: A turkey that plucks himself.

☼ ☼ ☼

Iggy: Where do all the bugs go in the winter?
Ziggy: Search me.
Iggy: No, thanks. I just wanted to know.

☼ ☼ ☼

Rich: What do you call a cat who likes to eat
   lemons?
Arianne: A sourpuss.

※ ※ ※

Page: What do you get when you cross a cat with a
   hyena?
Luke: A gigglepuss.

※ ※ ※

Trent: What do you call a cat who's joined the Red
   Cross?
Mary: A first-aid kit.

※ ※ ※

Donna: What does it mean if you go home and you
   don't have to do any chores or homework?
Jerry: It means you're in the wrong house.

※ ※ ※

Mark: Who is ringing the doorbell?
Christy: It is someone who is selling beehives.
Mark: Tell him to buzz off.

※ ※ ※

Nellie: How do they keep flies out of the kitchen in the school cafeteria?

Willie: They let them taste the food.

☀ ☀ ☀

Ned: Why did you quit your job at the bubble gum factory?

Jed: I bit off more then I could chew.

☀ ☀ ☀

Bruce: I just swallowed a pumpkin seed.

Ian: Don't worry about it. You'll be vine.

☀ ☀ ☀

Fuzzy: Last night I put my tooth under my pillow. This morning I found a dime there instead.

Wuzzy: When I put mine under my pillow, I got a dollar.

Fuzzy: Well, you have buck teeth.

☀ ☀ ☀

Matt: How much money do you have with you?

Jeff: Oh, between 48 dollars and 50 dollars.

Matt: Isn't that a lot of money to be carrying around?

Jeff: No, two dollars isn't much.

✷ ✷ ✷

Gus: Who is the nastiest Disney character?
Gabriel: Beats me.
Gus: Meanie Mouse.

✷ ✷ ✷

Annie: Did you hear about the cat who swallowed a
　　ball of yarn?
Jake: No, tell me.
Annie: She had mittens.

✷ ✷ ✷

Emily: My uncle swallowed a pound of chicken
　　feathers.
Lacey: What happened to him?
Emily: He was tickled to death.

✷ ✷ ✷

Sunny: My brother doesn't know how to cook.
Barry: How can you tell?
Sunny: Because last night he burned the salad.

✷ ✷ ✷

Geraldine: Who are the most despised football
    players?
Gaspar: I'm in the dark.
Geraldine: The offensive team.

☼ ☼ ☼

Ronald: Hey, did you hear the joke about Mars?
Dorothy: Yeah, it's far out!

Definitions

Academia nuts: Perpetual scholars.

✹ ✹ ✹

Antiques: Merchandise sold for old times' sake.

✹ ✹ ✹

Appeal: What a banana comes in.

✹ ✹ ✹

Arrange: Kitchen and cowboy necessity.

✹ ✹ ✹

Beastly weather: Raining cats and dogs.

✹ ✹ ✹

Cartoon: A song about an automobile.

☼ ☼ ☼

Coincide: What you should do when it rains.

☼ ☼ ☼

Compliment: The applause that refreshes.

☼ ☼ ☼

Icicle: An eavesdropper.

☼ ☼ ☼

Locomotive: Crazy impulse.

☼ ☼ ☼

Mistletoe: Platform base for a warhead.

☼ ☼ ☼

Monopoly: One parrot.

☼ ☼ ☼

Negate: A low swinging joint.

☼ ☼ ☼

Nobility: Unable to keep up due to a lack of aptitude.

☼ ☼ ☼

Nomad: Even-tempered.

☼ ☼ ☼

Parachutes: Double-barrel shotgun.

☼ ☼ ☼

Realize: Not glass peepers.

☼ ☼ ☼

Stork: The bird with the big bill.

☼ ☼ ☼

Surfeit: Ride the waves.

☼ ☼ ☼

Toadstool: A place for a frog to sit down.

☼ ☼ ☼

Unaware: Great-granddad's BVDs.

☼ ☼ ☼

Vanguard: Shotgun rider for moving company.

Reba & Regis

Reba: What do you call an X that just got out of the bathtub?
Regis: Search me.
Reba: A clean X.

☼ ☼ ☼

Reba: What do you call it when it rains chickens, ducks, and turkeys?
Regis: I'm in the dark.
Reba: Fowl weather.

☼ ☼ ☼

Reba: What do you get when you cross a rabbit with a spider?
Regis: I don't have the foggiest.
Reba: A hare net.

❂ ❂ ❂

Reba: What chicken was a famous American patriot?
Regis: I'm blank.
Reba: Pat-chick Henry.

❂ ❂ ❂

Reba: What did the rooster say when he saw Humpty-Dumpty fall?
Regis: That's a mystery.
Reba: Crack-a-doodle-doo.

❂ ❂ ❂

Reba: What are pants with a rip in them called?
Regis: I have no idea.
Reba: Van Winkle trousers.

❂ ❂ ❂

Reba: What animal goes "baa-baa-woof"?
Regis: I don't know.
Reba: A sheepdog.

❂ ❂ ❂

Reba: What is white and green and Irish and only comes out in the summer?

Regis: I pass.

Reba: Why, it's Paddy O'Furniture.

☀ ☀ ☀

Reba: What do they call a very fat tree limb?

Regis: Beats me.

Reba: Porky Twig.

☀ ☀ ☀

Reba: What did the limestone deposit say to the geologist?

Regis: My mind is a blank.

Reba: "You must stop taking me for granite."

☀ ☀ ☀

Reba: What is the shortest month in a year?

Regis: Who knows?

Reba: May. It only has three letters.

☀ ☀ ☀

Reba: What do bumblebees sing in the shower?

Regis: I give up.

Reba: Beebop.

☼ ☼ ☼

Reba: What kind of cookie breaks easily?
Regis: You tell me.
Reba: Gingersnaps.

☼ ☼ ☼

Reba: Where do you bathe?
Regis: I have no clue.
Reba: I said where, not when.

☼ ☼ ☼

Reba: What did the little lobster get on its math
    test?
Regis: I can't guess.
Reba: Sea-plus.

☼ ☼ ☼

Reba: What is green and goes up and down?
Regis: Search me.
Reba: A pickle in an elevator.

☼ ☼ ☼

Reba: What would you do if you broke a tooth
   while flossing?
Regis: I'm in the dark.
Reba: Use toothpaste.

☀ ☀ ☀

Reba: What is purple and divides the United States
   from Canada?
Regis: I don't have the foggiest.
Reba: The Grape Lakes.

☀ ☀ ☀

Reba: What would you be if a shark was in your
   bathtub?
Regis: I'm blank.
Reba: Chicken of the sea.

Far-out Answers

Q: How can you tell you are in bed with an anteater?
A: He has an A on his pajamas.

☼ ☼ ☼

Q: How do you keep a person from sleepwalking?
A: Spread tacks all over the floor.

☼ ☼ ☼

Q: How can you tell if there has been a hippopotamus in your refrigerator?
A: You can see his footprints in the butter.

☼ ☼ ☼

Q: How is the moon held up?
A: With moonbeams, I think.

☀ ☀ ☀

Q: How did the boo-tician style the ghost's hair?
A: With a scare dryer.

☀ ☀ ☀

Q: How can you tell that a leopard just took a bath?
A: He's spotless.

☀ ☀ ☀

Q: How do you make a kangaroo stew?
A: Keep him waiting for three hours.

☀ ☀ ☀

Q: How do you make antifreeze?
A: Hide her nightgown.

☀ ☀ ☀

Q: How do astronauts take their kids to school?
A: In space station wagons.

☀ ☀ ☀

Q: How did the jewel thief wake up every morning?
A: To a burglar alarm.

☀ ☀ ☀

Q: How do you take attendance in a bakery?
A: By roll call.

☀ ☀ ☀

Q: How do they make a Venetian blind?
A: Stick a finger in his eye.

☀ ☀ ☀

Q: How do you start a flea race?
A: One, two, flea, go!

☀ ☀ ☀

Q: How do you make gold soup?
A: Add 14 karats.

☀ ☀ ☀

Q: How do you know if your pizza can count?
A: Ask it how much 6 minus 6 is, and if it says
   nothing, you know it can count.

☀ ☀ ☀

Other Books by Bob Phillips

For more information, send a self-addressed
stamped envelope to:

Family Services
P.O. Box 9363
Fresno, California 93702